THIS IS MY BODY

BY GINA AND MERCER MAYER

Reader's Digest **Kids**

Westport, Connecticut

This is my body. It has different parts.
They all work together.

This is my fur. It keeps me warm,
especially in the wintertime.

When my fur gets too long, my mom takes me to the barber for a furcut. If I sit really still, I get a special treat.

These are my eyes.
They help me to see.

I use them to see
a little green worm . . .

to see a big tree . . .

and to see my dad
when he comes home
from work. "Hi, Dad!"

Sometimes I have to use my eyes
to watch my little brother. I don't like
to use them for that, though.

These are my ears.
They help me to hear.

I can hear when my dog barks.
That means someone's here.

I can also hear when my mom
asks me to clean my room.
Then I wish I didn't hear so well.

This is my nose.
It helps me to smell.

I can smell
Mom's perfume.

I can smell
my shampoo.

I can smell when my dog
has been playing with
a skunk! Ugh!

This is my mouth.

I use it to eat and to talk.
Dad says I talk all the time.
I guess I just have a lot to say.

These are my teeth.

They help me to chew
things I like . . .

and sometimes things
I don't really like.

I brush my teeth every night
to keep them clean.

This is my tummy.

This is where the food goes after I eat.

Sometimes if I eat too much sweet stuff
I get a tummy ache. That's why Mom
won't let me eat a whole bag of cookies.

These are my arms and hands.
I use them all the time.

They help me to turn
cartwheels . . .

to steer my bike . . .

and to turn pages of a book.

When I lasso a dinosaur, they help me
tie him up. They help me do
just about everything.

Especially take my toys back from my sister.

These are my elbows.

I use them to prop up my head when I'm sleepy.

These are my
legs and feet.

I use them to walk

. . . and climb.

When my sister is bothering me,
I use my legs and feet to run away from her.

These are my knees.
They help my legs bend.

When I fall down, my knees
always get banged up.

All the parts of my body work together
so I can do anything I want.

Everyone's body looks different,
but I think that's what makes us all special.